Jim and Jam have a Party

this is **Jim**

in every picture look for his pet mouse **Jam**

Written and devised by Angela Littler
Illustrated by Anita McEwen

HODDER AND STOUGHTON
LONDON   SYDNEY   AUCKLAND   TORONTO

Jim wants his friends
to come to his birthday party.
He is writing the invitations.
It takes a long time.

☆ Jim's invitation cards have clown faces on them.
Can you find four cards? Are they all the same?

● Help Jim to find four envelopes for his cards.

The great day comes!
Jim says hello to everybody.
They give him presents.
Three presents are the same.
They are all water pistols.

 Can you find these things in the picture?

long green balloon

2 round red balloons   3 blue and white cups   4 four's    5 yellow spoons

Jim has a good idea.
He can use all his presents.
They all go outside
to play his new game.
Jam plays, too.

☆ The ball must go LEFT round the first post, RIGHT round the second one and THROUGH the goal. Trace the way with your finger.

- In which hand is Jim holding the water pistol?
- Can you disentangle the two skipping ropes?
- Look around. What other games can they play?

They play lots of games indoors.
Now they are looking for
hidden lollipops.
Finders keepers!

☆ Can you help the children find these lollipops?

Time for tea!
There are good things to eat.
Jim blows out the candles
on his cake.

☆ Jim gave everyone a number for a place at the table. Are they all sitting in the right seats?

- How old is Jim? How do you know?
- Count how many little cakes, sausages and sandwiches are left.

Jam jumps up suddenly.
He makes Jim drop
the lemonade jug.
Look out everybody!

☆ Where are all the little cakes, sausages and sandwiches now?

- Two children threw streamers. Can you see where they landed?
- Follow each streamer with your finger.

Nobody is hurt,
but the table is a mess.
They all help tidy up.
Jam has his own party
under the table.

 Jim and his friends did some puzzles.
Can you fit in the last pieces for them?

- Have they cleaned all the food off the floor?

After tea,
everybody goes home.
They all have a balloon.
The party was fun.
Goodbye Jim! Goodbye Jam!

☆ Who owns which balloon?
Trace the strings with your finger.

- One girl has lost her balloon. Can you help her find it?

Word and Picture Puzzle

 present    ball    card

 cake   spoon    envelope

 candle    cup    jug

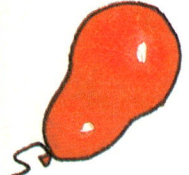 balloon    lollipop    plate

Look at these pictures and read the words several times. Try putting a strip of paper (or a coin, or your hand) over the pictures. Now can your read what each word says?

Squirt Game

You can play this game in the bath, or outdoors with a bowl of water. Make goalposts in the water with two plastic straws. (Stick the straws into blobs of plasticine to make them stand firm).

Now fill an empty washing-up liquid bottle with water and push the squirt top back on. Float a ping pong ball in the bath or bowl, aim your bottle at the ball – and squeeze! You will soon find out how to guide the ball with the stream of water. The first person to get a goal, wins. Make the goalposts narrower as you get more skilful.

Things to do at your Party

1. Stick the Nose on the Clown

Draw a huge picture of a clown and colour it in. Make a cross where his nose should be. Stick the picture up on the wall. Then blindfold each guest in turn and give them a sticky-backed spot (you can buy packs of them from stationers). They must try to stick the spot as close as possible to the cross on the clown's nose. Remember to put each person's name on their spot when they have finished. The one nearest the cross wins.

2. Freeze!

Play some music, and ask everyone to dance round the room. Keep stopping the music suddenly. When it stops, all the dancers must 'freeze'. Anyone who moves is out.

3. Play Dead

Everyone lies very still on the floor. Anyone who moves is out. To make the game more fun, try saying some silly things to make people laugh and catch them out.

4. Pass the Balloon

Use two sausage-shaped balloons. Make up two teams. On the word 'Go!', each team passes their balloon from the person at the back of the team to the one at the front. There is only one catch – you must pass the balloon with your elbows only!

5. Paper Plate Masks

This is good sit-down fun when everyone is tired. Get a grown-up to prepare lots of plain white paper plates by cutting eye and nose holes in them, and attaching string or elastic to each side. Collect lots of bits and pieces before the party, such as tissue paper scraps (to scrunch up for flowers), cotton wool balls (for hair), stick-on spots, ribbons, glitter, felt-tip pens, etc. Put them all out with some children's glue (the sticks of glue are the least messy). Now everyone can make a face mask.

Goal!

A game for 2-4 players. You will need a dice, and a counter for each player.

Start at the bottom, throw the dice and move your counter on plain-coloured balls only, until you reach 'finish'. Do not move your counter on to patterned balls. Do not move on to someone else's ball. You can move in any direction on to any plain ball, as long as it is touching the ball you are on. The first person to finish the game and score a goal is the winner.